NATIONS of the NORTHWEST COAST

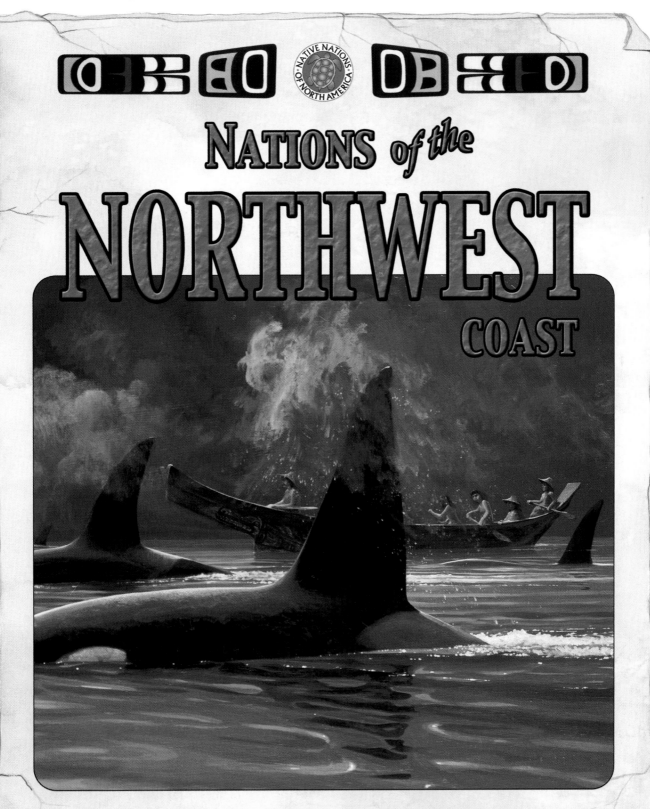

Kathryn Smithyman & Bobbie Kalman
Crabtree Publishing Company
www.crabtreebooks.com

NATIONS of the
NORTHWEST
COAST

Created by Bobbie Kalman

Dedicated by Kathryn Smithyman
For the BACL:AVA - with my love

Editor-in-Chief
Bobbie Kalman

Writing team
Kathryn Smithyman
Bobbie Kalman

Substantive editor
Niki Walker

Editors
Molly Aloian
Amanda Bishop
Rebecca Sjonger

Art director
Robert MacGregor

Design
Margaret Amy Reiach

Production coordinator
Heather Fitzpatrick

Photo research
Crystal Foxton
Laura Hysert

Consultant
Michael Marker, Ph.D., Associate Professor, Department
    of Educational Studies, University of British Columbia

Photographs and reproductions
© American Museum of Natural History Library: page 29
Bill Holm: front cover, pages 6 (top), 15, 18, 22, 27
Courtesy Canadian Museum of Civilization, artist Gordon Miller,
    1997, image no. S99-12621: page 12
Carl Stromquist (Interior Salish), *Brotherhood, Edition of 170*: page 31
Illustrations by Gordon Miller: pages 1, 5, 6 (bottom), 8-9, 14, 19, 20,
    21, 23 (top-left & bottom), 26, 30
© Permission of Lazare & Parker: page 10
National Archives of Canada/C-114482/C-114475, Bushnell
    Collection: page 28
Greg Harlin, National Geographic Society Image Collection: page 16
With Permission of the Royal Ontario Museum © ROM: pages
    23 (top-right), 25
Other images by Digital Stock

Illustrations
Barbara Bedell: pages 3, 7 (bottom), 10 (bottom), 11 (bottom), 13, 15,
    17 (bottom), 20, 24 (bear)
Katherine Kantor: border, pages 4 (map of Northwest Coast), 24 (map)
Margaret Amy Reiach: back cover, pages 7 (top), 11 (top), 16,
    17 (top & middle), 21, 22, 23, 30
Bonna Rouse: page 4 (map of North America)

Crabtree Publishing Company
www.crabtreebooks.com   1-800-387-7650

PMB 16A	612 Welland Avenue	73 Lime Walk
350 Fifth Avenue	St. Catharines	Headington
Suite 3308	Ontario	Oxford
New York, NY	Canada	OX3 7AD
10118	L2M 5V6	United Kingdom

Cataloging-in-Publication Data
Smithyman, Kathryn.
    Nations of the Northwest Coast / Kathryn Smithyman &
Bobbie Kalman.
        p. cm. -- (Native nations of North America series)
Includes index.
Summary: Explores how the waters, mountains, and forests of
the Pacific Northwest have provided food and shelter for groups
such as the Tlingit, the Haida, and the Kwakiutl for thousands of
years.
    ISBN 0-7787-0378-9 (lib. bdg. : alk. paper) -- ISBN 0-7787-0470-X
(pbk. : alk. paper)
    1. Indians of North America--Northwest Coast of North
America--History--Juvenile literature. 2. Indians of North
America--Northwest Coast of North America--Social life and
customs--Juvenile literature. [1. Indians of North America--
Northwest Coast of North America.] I. Kalman, Bobbie, 1947- II.
Title. III. Series.
    E78.N78S56 2003
    979.5004'97--dc22
                                                        2003016194
                                                                LC

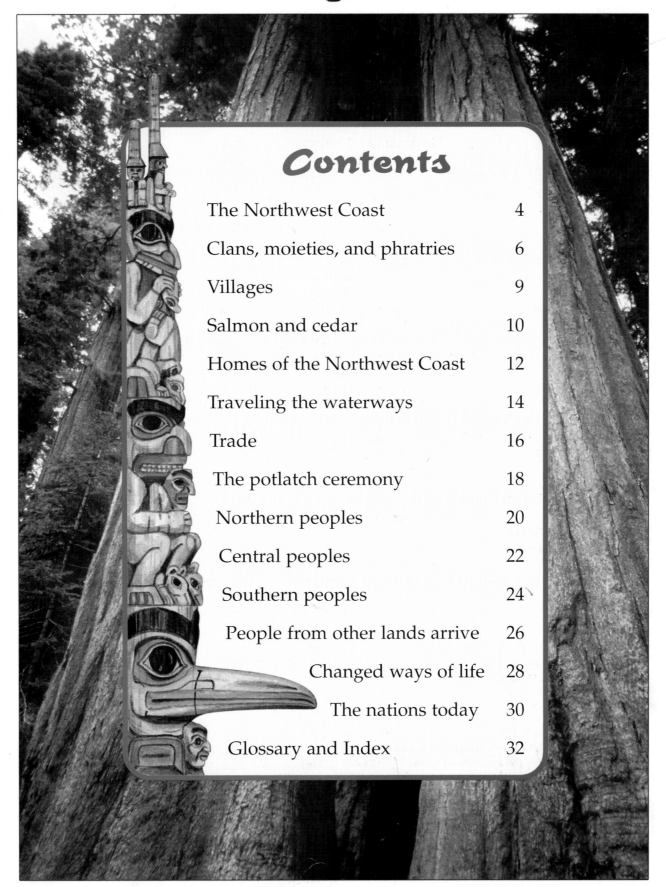

Contents

The Northwest Coast

Indigenous, or Native, peoples have lived in the Northwest Coast region of North America for at least 11,000 years. This region stretches about 2,000 miles (3219 km) along the Pacific Ocean from the northern part of present-day California to the southern part of present-day Alaska. The region is a narrow strip of land—less than 100 miles (161 km) wide in most places—that lies between the ocean and the Coast Mountains. The Northwest Coast region also includes hundreds of islands.

Lush rainforests

The region's **climate** is mild and wet. In many places, more than 100 inches (254 cm) of rain falls each year. Warm temperatures and plentiful rain help lush **rainforests** grow. Red cedars, yellow cedars, and spruce trees reach towering heights in these forests.

Land of plenty
The ocean and the region's rivers and forests provided the Native peoples with all the food and **natural resources**, or materials from nature, that they needed. The waters teemed with shellfish, whales, seals, sea lions, sea otters, and many kinds of fish. The forests offered foods such as roots and berries, as well as materials such as wood and bark.

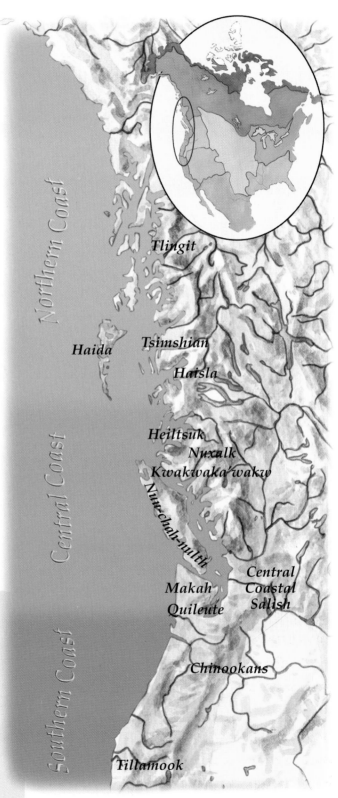

The Northwest Coast region can be divided into Northern, Central, and Southern areas.

4

Many peoples

Native peoples of the Northwest Coast lived in hundreds of separate villages. The people in each community had their own languages, customs, and traditions. They also had **territories**, or areas surrounding their villages where they fished, hunted, and collected natural resources. People from different villages gathered for celebrations, traded with one another, and, sometimes, fought wars. Eventually, many neighboring groups developed similar languages and cultures.

Today, people that live in the same region and have similar languages are considered one **nation**. For example, more than thirty villages of people who speak a version of the Kwakiutl language are now known as the Kwakwaka'wakw nation. The map on page 4 shows where many of the Northwest Coast nations lived. Although this book discusses the lives of Northwest Coast peoples as they lived in the past, many of their **descendants** still live in the same areas and maintain the values, beliefs, and traditions described here.

Clans, moieties, and phratries

The people in each village were organized into important groups. **Clans** were family groups that were part of larger village groups called **moieties** and **phratries**. A moiety divided a village into two groups, whereas a phratry separated villagers into four groups.

Part of a clan

Some villages had only two clans; other villages had several clans. Belonging to a clan was an essential part of a person's life. Children were born into the clans of their parents, usually those of the mothers. Although the members of a clan were not always blood relatives, they thought of themselves as "brothers" and "sisters." Members of the same clan could not marry one another. Clans in the same moiety or phratry were also related. As a result, two people from the same moiety or phratry could not marry.

Clan ancestry

The people in a clan believed that they all shared the same spirit **ancestor**. The spirit was that of a respected animal such as a raven, eagle, orca, or wolf, or a **mythical** being such as the thunderbird.

The Tlingit leader above is dressed in ceremonial clothing that displays his high rank.

The Haida and some other peoples consider the raven to be one of their ancestors.

Clan property

A clan's **property** was made up of the group's belongings. It could never be used by anyone who was not a clan member. Each clan had its own houses, fishing spots, and berry-picking areas, as well as songs, stories, and ceremonies describing its history and ancestors, and a **crest**. A clan's crest was a symbol that represented its spirit ancestor. It was carved or painted on many items that people made. Clan property and resources belonged to all clan members, but they were controlled by the clan's **chief**, or leader.

Inheriting a place

Privileges, rights, and roles were important to all peoples of the Northwest Coast. Their roles in clans and communities were **inherited**, or passed on from their ancestors. A clan chief, for example, was the leader because his ancestors had been clan leaders before him. The leader of the largest or highest-ranking clan was the chief of the entire community.

Ranking people

Most Northwest Coast clans had three **ranks** of people—**nobles**, **commoners**, and **slaves**. Clan chiefs and their relatives were nobles. They were the wealthiest members of their clans. Most chiefs and nobles did not have to fish, hunt, or gather resources because commoners and slaves did much of this work. Commoners were respected members of a community but were of lower rank than the nobles. They had fewer inherited rights and less wealth. Slaves, who were owned by nobles and clan leaders, had no rights. Most were captured during raids on other villages. The children of slaves also became slaves.

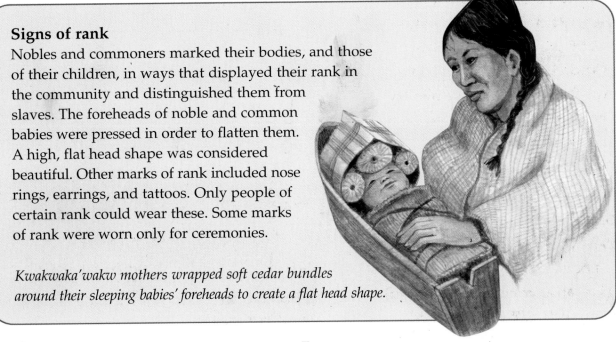

Signs of rank

Nobles and commoners marked their bodies, and those of their children, in ways that displayed their rank in the community and distinguished them from slaves. The foreheads of noble and common babies were pressed in order to flatten them. A high, flat head shape was considered beautiful. Other marks of rank included nose rings, earrings, and tattoos. Only people of certain rank could wear these. Some marks of rank were worn only for ceremonies.

Kwakwaka'wakw mothers wrapped soft cedar bundles around their sleeping babies' foreheads to create a flat head shape.

Villages

Villages in the Northwest Coast region were made up of large houses shared by many people. Some villages had only a single house, but most had about a dozen houses. The largest villages had as many as 40 houses. All the houses were built in rows facing the ocean.

House groups

Each house was home to as many as 100 people. Together, these people formed a **house group**. The owners of each house were nobles. They were descendants of the people who had owned the house before them. Commoners were part of a house group because they were related to the owners or because they worked for them. Slaves also lived in the house.

Seasonal camps

Although people lived in permanent villages, many traveled around their territories to gather food and resources from spring until fall. They saved some of the food for use during winter, when hunting and gathering could be difficult. Most groups had several clan-owned fishing, hunting, and gathering spots within their territories. People set up camps at various sites throughout the year. They returned to the same campsites year after year.

Northwest Coast villages, such as this Haida village at Masset, were built right near the ocean's shore.

Salmon and cedar

People took great care to respect resources by using them wisely. They never took more animals or plants than they needed and did not fish or hunt during the times when animals were **breeding**.

Although the Northwest Coast was rich in a variety of natural resources, two of these—salmon and cedar—were both plentiful and important to the Native peoples. Salmon provided much of their food, and cedar was used to make useful objects. Most of the groups that lived along this coast based their livelihoods on the goods they could produce with cedar. They kept the goods they needed and traded the **surplus**, or extra, for other items (see pages 16-17).

Time of the salmon

Salmon was a highly valued resource. Many groups held ceremonies to thank the spirit of the salmon at the beginning of every **salmon run**. A salmon run took place during a few weeks each year, when millions of these fish swam upstream from the ocean into rivers to lay eggs. As the fish swam up the rivers, men caught large numbers with spears, nets, or traps called **weirs**. Women gathered salmon eggs, which was another favorite food.

Other types of food

Most groups caught fish and ocean animals for food. They also gathered shellfish, such as clams, barnacles, and scallops, which washed up onto shore. In the nearby forests, people searched for bird eggs, plants, and animals to eat. Depending on the region, hunters tracked deer, beavers, caribou, or bears.

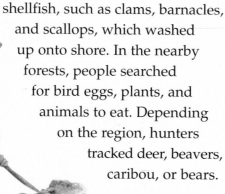

Women used sticks to uncover clams along beaches.

Food for later

Women were responsible for cleaning the salmon that were caught. They also cooked some of the fish. Most of the salmon, however, was **preserved** to be eaten in the months to come.

Useful cedar

Northwest Coast peoples made many items from cedar, including houses and canoes (see pages 12-15). Woodworkers also crafted household items such as storage chests, benches, bowls, dishes, spoons, ladles, tools, and weapons. Some of these items were carved into beautiful shapes or decorated with designs to honor spirits.

Versatile bark

Cedar trees have bark that is made up of two thick layers—outer bark and inner bark. The hard outer bark was used to make items such as boxes, bowls, canoe bailers, and small huts. People also used narrow strips of outer bark as **twine**, or string, on which rows of fish were hung to dry.

Clothed in bark

The inner bark of cedar trees was soft and stringy. Native women shredded the bark into strips that could be woven to make baskets, hats, blankets, mats, skirts, and capes. Shredded bark could also be **soft-shredded**, or shredded until it formed hairlike strands. Soft-shredded bark was used to weave soft diapers, towels, and fringes for blankets and clothing.

Northwest Coast peoples saw that bark was the perfect "clothing" for trees and believed that it was also perfect for their own clothing.

Homes of the Northwest Coast

The weather along the Northwest Coast is mild most of the year, but winters often bring storms with harsh winds and pounding rains. People had to build sturdy homes to withstand these conditions. They built **plankhouses** using cedar. Cedar was the best wood to use because it split easily into long, straight **planks** and was slow to **rot**, or decay, in wet weather. The plankhouses in one village sometimes looked different from those in other villages, but most homes were built in the same way. Builders made rectangular frames with cedar logs and then used planks to construct the walls, roof, and floor. Inside, each house was divided into private spaces by mats of woven cedar bark that hung from the ceiling. Plank shelves ran along the walls and were used as sleeping platforms or as storage spaces. Most homes had a large fire pit in the middle of the floor.

Roof planks fit together snugly to keep out the rain, but they were not attached to the buildings. The planks could be moved to let in light or to let out smoke. Heavy stones kept the planks in place during storms.

Longhouses

People who lived in the southern part of the region built plankhouses with **shed roofs**. These roofs sloped down from the front of the building to the back of the building, as shown below. Often, one house was built against the side of another house or attached to a group of shed-roofed houses. Together, these dwellings formed a long line of adjoining houses that was sometimes called a **longhouse**.

Camp houses

At their seasonal camps, people set up several structures, including shelters and storage huts. Camp structures often looked like small, roughly built plankhouses. People constructed them by laying cedar planks over pole frames. They brought the cedar planks from their villages and took the planks with them when they departed. They usually left the pole frames standing from year to year, however.

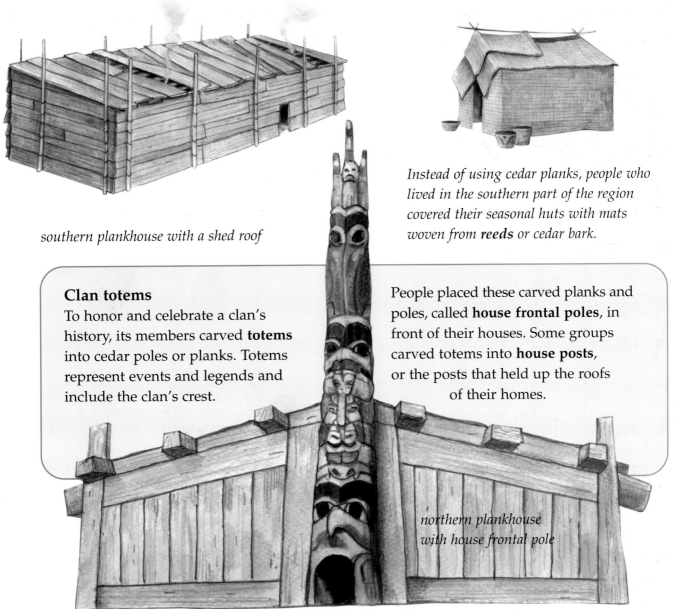

southern plankhouse with a shed roof

*Instead of using cedar planks, people who lived in the southern part of the region covered their seasonal huts with mats woven from **reeds** or cedar bark.*

Clan totems

To honor and celebrate a clan's history, its members carved **totems** into cedar poles or planks. Totems represent events and legends and include the clan's crest.

People placed these carved planks and poles, called **house frontal poles**, in front of their houses. Some groups carved totems into **house posts**, or the posts that held up the roofs of their homes.

northern plankhouse with house frontal pole

Traveling the waterways

The Northwest Coast region has many rivers and streams that flow into one another and eventually empty into the Pacific Ocean. The people who lived there understood this network of waterways and used it to travel from place to place. Even when people needed to reach a forest to hunt or gather food, they usually traveled to the site by canoe rather than walking to it overland. Most forests were so thick that moving through them was difficult. It was easier to paddle a canoe to a shore near the site and then walk a short distance to it.

Northwest Coast canoes were carved from a single log. Long canoes with high fronts were made to cut through ocean waves. Their shape made paddling less difficult.

Types of canoes

Every village had hundreds of canoes of various shapes and sizes. Each was designed for a specific job and waterway. Canoes used for ocean travel were made in many styles. Whale-hunting vessels had to be especially stable in the water. These sturdy boats were up to 70 feet (21 m) long and held 30 or more men. **Freight canoes** were were about 40 feet (12 m) long, seven feet (2 m) wide, and held up to five tons (5080 kg) of cargo. They were designed to carry a lot of weight and were used to transport food and supplies from one place to another. A freight canoe, for example, was used to haul loads of salmon from a fishing camp to a village.

People who lived near streams often made flat-bottomed canoes, which they steered through shallow waters using long poles.

When people needed to move large loads, they piled them onto cedar planks that were laid across two freight canoes.

Each family had a general-purpose canoe, such as this Coastal Salish family's boat.

Trade

Along the Northwest Coast, trade was an ancient tradition. Trading allowed groups to acquire the goods, foods, and resources that were not available near their villages. Sometimes, members of two communities traded with one another. At other times, people from many villages met to trade. Every spring, traders from all along the coast gathered at the mouth of the Nass River in present-day British Columbia. Each group had items that were of particular value. By the 1700s, some Native groups, such as the Nuu-chah-nulth shown left, acquired goods from Europeans and Russians, which they then traded to Native people in other communities.

Trading was always carried out with respect. Traders believed they increased their people's honor if they made valuable trades.

Trade with inland peoples

The Coast Mountains separated most Northwest Coast groups from people outside the region. A few groups, however, were able to trade with people who lived farther inland. The Tlingit acquired fur and copper by trading with communities in the north and to the east. The Coastal Salish also did a great deal of trading with peoples to the east. The Chinookans held huge trade gatherings, where they obtained goods such as furs, skins, mountain-goat wool, and tobacco from groups who lived east of the mountains.

Valuable items

Some groups had large quantities of goods or very valuable items to trade. These people became wealthy. Many groups gained great wealth by trading resources that were available only in their territories. Some of these resources were needed to make everyday items, but many were valued for their beauty or because they were rare.

The Makah hunted whales and traded whale oil to people who did not hunt whales. The oil was used to prepare and preserve foods.

*The Nuu-chah-nulth traded small horn-shaped shells, called **dentalia** shells, which washed ashore in their territory. Many groups used the shells as beads.*

Highly prized canoes

The Haida were particularly skilled canoe-makers. Haida canoes were beautifully carved and painted, as shown right. The Haida made extra canoes, which they traded along the Northwest Coast. The canoes were crafted with such skill that some peoples, such as the Tlingit, stopped making large freight canoes for themselves. They used only Haida freight canoes, for which they exchanged many goods. Most Haida groups were very wealthy, partly because of the huge number of goods they received for a single canoe.

The potlatch ceremony

Most of the Northwest Coast peoples believed that powerful spirits lived in the ocean, in the forests, and in the air. The people believed that everything they had, including their wealth and their rank in society, was due to the generosity of these spirits. People honored the spirits and showed gratitude through various ceremonies. Some ceremonies included the entire village; others involved select groups of people. Most ceremonies were held in winter, when the spirits were thought to move closer to the people and sometimes even show themselves.

One important ceremony was the **potlatch**. The potlatch was a gift-giving ceremony in which a host treated guests to food, singing, and dancing. The host and his guests wore ceremonial clothing, which included elaborate robes that showed their clan crests. Potlatches were held to celebrate a variety of occasions. Some marked important events in a person's life, such as a marriage or the birth of a child. Others honored clan members who had died. Potlatches that celebrated family events were held both by nobles and by commoners.

A Tlingit chief greets his guests as they arrive for a potlatch. The word "potlatch" comes from a Nuu-chah-nulth word, "patshatl," which means "sharing."

A celebration of status

A chief also hosted a special potlatch ceremony in order to confirm and celebrate his status. At this type of potlatch, songs, dances, and speeches told stories of the chief's ancestors to reinforce his rank and inherited rights. The potlatch was planned far in advance, and the entire community was involved in the preparations. Chiefs and nobles from other villages were invited to attend, and these guests brought their entire house groups. The potlatch lasted for days or even weeks. It included elaborate feasts and generous gifts from the host to his guests. Gift-giving allowed a chief to display his wealth as well as his generosity.

People performed songs and dances using ceremonial masks to represent their spirit ancestors. Potlatches were one way people such as the Tlingit, above, showed respect for themselves, their guests, and the spirits that were important in their lives.

Northern peoples

The Haida, the Tlingit, and the Tsimshian nations lived in the northern coast area (see map on page 4). Each nation was made up of several communities. People in each community lived according to their own traditions. Each village spoke a **dialect**, or version, of their nation's language. People in various Haida communities, for example, spoke different dialects of the Haida language.

The Haida

The people known today as the Haida were once at least six separate communities. Most were located on Haida Gwaii, which is a group of more than 200 islands. The name "Haida Gwaii" means "Islands of the People." The Haida depended heavily on ocean animals for food, since only a few types of plants and animals were available on the islands. From early in their history, these people were aggressive warriors who raided surrounding villages—both on the islands and on the mainland. From some groups, they took goods and slaves by force, but they traded peacefully with others. Haida woodworkers carved animal designs into useful items with a unique style that many people found very attractive. Their canoes and other carved items were popular for trade.

The Kaigani

One group of Haida—the Kaigani—lived on the coast near the present-day border between Alaska and British Columbia. Their territory included forests that were home to deer, beavers, minks, and water birds. The Kaigani ate more forest plants and animals than did most other northern groups.

The Tlingit

The name "Tlingit" means "human beings" in the Tlingit language. The Tlingit included sixteen independent groups, one of which was the Chilkat. Tlingit territory was located in what is now known as the Alaska Panhandle. The territory was about 500 miles (805 km) long and no more than 30 miles (48 km) wide. Tlingit hunters caught many land animals, including deer, bears, caribou, mountain sheep, and mountain goats. Chilkat women used the wool of mountain goats to weave a unique type of blanket. The Chilkat wore them as ceremonial robes, but the blankets were also valued trade items.

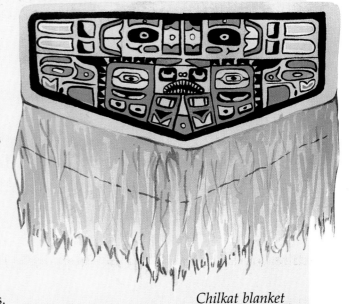

Chilkat blanket

The Tsimshian

In ancient times, the Tsimshian were not located in the northern coast area. Historians believe they settled in present-day British Columbia in the 1700s. Their arrival forced the Tlingit to move farther north. The Tsimshian gathered plants and hunted animals in the surrounding forests, but they relied mainly on fish for food. Early each spring, schools of tiny fish called eulachon entered the rivers in Tsimshian territory to spawn. The oil from eulachon was very useful and was a valuable trade item. The Tsimshian dried and pressed the fish to extract the oil or boiled the fish and skimmed the oil from the top of the water. They seasoned their food with the oil and used it to preserve foods. They also traded the oil or "grease" with other peoples, who used it as a spread on their food.

Central peoples

Many nations lived in the central coast area. They included the Makah, the Nuu-chah-nulth, the Kwakwaka'wakw, the Heiltsuk, the Haisla, and the Nuxalk. Although rank and inherited rights were important to these peoples, most displayed fewer crests and other clan markings than the northern groups did. Two groups—the Makah and the Nuu-chah-nulth—were **whalers**, or whale hunters. People all along the Northwest Coast used **stranded** whales for their blubber, but only the Makah and the Nuu-chah-nulth hunted whales for food. Whale hunting was a dangerous activity requiring courage, strength, and fitness.

whaling hat

The Makah
The Makah people lived on the northwest tip of the Olympic Peninsula in present-day Washington State. They call themselves "Qwidicca-atx," which means "people who live on the cape by the rocks and seagulls."

The Nuu-chah-nulth
The Nuu-chah-nulth lived in more than 22 villages along the western half of present-day Vancouver Island, in a place non-Natives called Nootka Sound. For many years, these people were incorrectly called "Nootkans."

The ability to hunt whales was a source of great pride to the Nuu-chah-nulth (shown above) and the Makah.

The Heiltsuk

The Heiltsuk lived in six communities in Waglisla, or Bella Bella, in present-day British Columbia. Non-Natives called these peoples "Bella Bella." The Heiltsuk had strong trade and family ties with the Nuxalk.

The Kwakwaka'wakw

"Kwakwaka'wakw" is the nation name for many groups whose territory was near Queen Charlotte Strait in present-day British Columbia. These groups are often mistakenly called "Kwakiutl," which is actually the name of their language. Kwakwaka'wakw carvers made large ceremonial masks—many with moving parts.

The Haisla

The Haisla lived at Kitamaat in present-day British Columbia. These peoples made and traded high-quality eulachon grease.

The Nuxalk

There were at least 45 communities located in a valley along the north shore of the Bella Coola River, in present-day British Columbia. The people living in these villages were known as the "Bella Coola" for many years, but they now refer to themselves as the Nuxalk nation.

Southern peoples

Many peoples lived in the southern part of the Northwest Coast region. Their main sources of food were found in the ocean, but many of their villages were located farther inland than those in other parts of the region. The villages were built among forests and **foothills**, or hills near the bases of mountains.

A different lifestyle

Although the peoples who lived in this area shared many of the lifeways of groups to the north, their lives differed in some important ways. One key difference was the climate of the area in which they lived. The weather in the south was mild, allowing people to hunt and gather food year round. Food was plentiful in the forests, and travel was easy, even in winter. People gathered a wide variety of plants and hunted forest animals such as deer, beavers, bears, otters, and groundhogs. They used the skins and furs of these animals to make clothing.

Only some of the southern coast nation names appear on this map. The labels show the territory of each nation. The Coastal Salish nations are made up of peoples from several smaller nations.

Pacific Ocean

Northern Coastal Salish

Central Coastal Salish

Lummi

Makah

Quileute

Chemakum

Swinomish

Quinault

Southern Coastal Salish

Southwestern Coastal Salish

Kwalhioqua

Chinookans

Clatskanie

Tillamook

Kalapuyans

Alseans

Siuslawans

Coosans

Athapaskans

Takelma

Different ranks

Some communities in the southern part of the region had a system of ranking people that was different than elsewhere on the Northwest Coast. There were more than three ranks, and the ranks were not fixed. In some communities, it was possible for a particularly talented person to move up to a higher rank. Sometimes slaves could earn their freedom if they perfomed a heroic feat, such as saving a noble's life.

Coastal Salish weaving

Coastal Salish weavers used a technique that was not used by any other peoples of the Northwest Coast. They made yarn by spinning the fur or hair from many types of animals, including dogs. The yarn was then woven to make clothing and blankets. These woven items were highly valued by traders from many nations.

The woman in the background, near the entranceway, is spinning yarn.

People from other lands arrive

Some historians believe that the first contact between Native peoples and outsiders took place in the 1600s, when a group of Russians traded with the Tlingit. The Russians acquired sea otter **pelts**, or furs, and sold them in China for large sums of money. In 1778, a British explorer named Captain James Cook realized that British companies could also make huge profits by selling furs in China. Word of the potential profits quickly spread, and competition for furs soon developed among Spanish, British, and American traders. A flood of non-Native hunters and traders in search of furs arrived in the Northwest Coast region. Most of the newcomers relied on Native people to hunt large numbers of animals. In exchange, they offered goods from Europe and Asia. The Northwest Coast groups were shrewd traders. They encouraged competition among the Europeans and would not exchange their pelts for trinkets. They valued only useful trade items such as guns, iron, sugar, flour, blankets, and sails that could be used on their canoes.

Native traders loaded their canoes and paddled out to the European ships, where the trading took place.

Chinookan "trade jargon"

When Europeans and Native people first met, they had difficulty understanding each other. Since both groups believed they would benefit from trading, they developed a way of communicating. A lot of trade took place in Chinookan territory, so Native and European traders developed a "trade jargon" based on the Chinookan language. It was made up of European pronunciations of Chinookan words. This trade jargon was used by European and Native traders all over the Northwest Coast.

A devastating result

European and Russian traders and explorers carried diseases such as smallpox, measles, and influenza. Native people, who had never encountered these diseases, had no natural defenses against them. The diseases spread quickly throughout Native communities, and many people became sick. More than three-quarters of all the Native people on the Northwest Coast died from newly introduced illnesses. In some cases, entire Native communities were wiped out. So many Native people died, that those who were left had no choice but to join together and live in central villages.

When Native people acquired European trade goods, such as buttons and wool blankets, they added the items to their clothing and traditions. For example, they used buttons to decorate blankets, which they then used to make ceremonial robes. These robes were called "button blankets."

Changed ways of life

By the late 1800s and early 1900s, it was becoming very difficult for Native people to live according to their traditional ways. The governments of Britain and the United States did not recognize Native people as legal owners of their lands or of the resources on them. As a result, Native people were not allowed to profit from the fish, trees, gold, and other resources that were taken from their lands.

The fishing business

Europeans and Americans caught huge numbers of fish to sell. They built **canneries**, or factories for canning the fish, on traditional Native lands. The factories attracted European and American workers, who built homes and farms on Native territories. Many Native people, especially those along the southern coast, were forced to leave their homes. Those who lived around present-day Seattle, Washington, and Vancouver, British Columbia, were affected the most by settlers occupying their territories.

Reserves and reservations

Many Native peoples were offered **treaties**, or agreements, that set aside land for their use. These lands were called **reservations** in the United States and **reserves** in Canada. They often included fishing and hunting areas but were rarely located on traditional homelands. Many groups refused to sign the treaties.

Altered traditions

As the populations in Native villages shrank and people from different villages were forced to live together, power struggles developed among chiefs. Sometimes men without inherited rights to leadership became chiefs of newly formed communities. Under new leadership, traditional ways often changed. In the 1800s, the American and Canadian governments made laws to prevent Native peoples from participating in ceremonies such as potlatches. The governments also passed laws that made it illegal for Native people to fish and hunt. Without their traditional lands and ways, Native people could not support their families. Many were forced to hold potlatches in secret and to take jobs in canning factories or in the logging industry that was quickly growing in the region.

Forced change

The American and Canadian governments forced Native parents to send their children to boarding schools far from their homes. At these schools, children were taught American or British and Canadian history and culture. The children were not allowed to speak their own languages, and teachers made them feel ashamed of their cultures. Parents who refused to send their children to boarding schools were punished. Their children were removed from their homes and adopted by American or Canadian families. By separating the children from their parents, governments attempted to destroy Native cultures.

The nations today

Today, thousands of Native people live along the Northwest Coast. Many nations have formed groups that work to raise awareness of their traditions, languages, beliefs, and ceremonies. Several colleges and universities have Native Studies programs. Both Native and non-Native students of all ages are encouraged to learn more about Native cultures. Several nations have their own schools, such as Salish Kootenai College, where people study traditional languages and cultures and earn degrees.

People from many nations have formed organizations that look after their rights and interests. Some work with governments to establish laws to protect forests, fish populations, and water sources. Some groups have helped create laws that ensure the equal treatment of their people. Many are working to regain their homelands and their rights to practice traditional customs such as whaling. The Makah nation, for example, has earned the right to catch up to five whales per year.

Bill Reid is a carver who learned the Haida carving style used by his ancestors. He carved the canoe shown above, which was the first traditional canoe in the region in more than 100 years. In 1987, chiefs from many nations joined the Haida to celebrate its arrival. Bill Reid stands in the bow of the canoe.

Celebrating traditions

Many peoples of the Northwest Coast are proud of their **heritage**. Their nations are still governed by **elders** and chiefs, who lead their people in ceremonies. Elders are older respected members of the nations. Artists continue to create the same types of items as those produced by their ancestors. The Haisla people, for example, continue to make and use eulachon grease. Contemporary artists such as Carl Stromquist carve, weave, or paint using traditional styles to celebrate the arts and crafts of the Northwest Coast. Stromquist is a Salish carver and painter. His painting entitled, *Brotherhood*, is shown below.

Find out more

If you are interested in learning more about the Native peoples of the Northwest Coast, there are many useful websites you can visit. Start with these:

- www.bcfn.org/culture.htm
- www.civilization.ca/aborig/haida/haindexe.html
- www.maltwood.uvic.ca/nwcp/central/intro.html (then click "begin game")

Glossary

Note: Boldfaced words that are defined in the book may not appear in the glossary.

ancestor An ancient relative or spirit animal from whom or from which someone is believed to be descended

breed To produce young

clan A group of people who are believed to share an animal spirit as their ancestor

climate The long-term weather conditions in an area, including temperature, rainfall, and wind

descendant A person who comes from a particular ancestor or group of ancestors

freight canoe A canoe used to move large loads of goods from place to place

heritage The history, traditions, and culture associated with one's ancestors

moiety One of two kinship groups that make up a Native society and are based on either the mothers' or fathers' family lines

mythical Describing a legendary story, person, or thing

nation A group of Native communities that live in the same region and share similar languages

phratry One of four kinship groups that make up a Native society and are based on either the mothers' or fathers' family lines

plank A thick flat wooden board

preserve To prepare foods so they will not spoil

rainforest A dense evergreen forest that receives at least 100 inches (254 cm) of rain each year

rank A person's position in society, which determines his or her rights or power

reed A tall grass with hollow stems

stranded Describing whales that swim onto shore and die when they cannot return to the ocean

totem 1. An animal believed to be the founder, ancestor, or guardian of a clan or family of Native peoples 2. An image or emblem showing the totem animal

Index

1 2 3 4 5 6 7 8 9 0   Printed in the U.S.A. 3 2 1 0 9 8 7 6 5 4